# The Shifting Nature of Weather

## Contents

# Predicting the Weather

The weather is always changing. It can be sunny and warm one day, then rainy and cold the next. Temperatures can rise or fall from day to day. Storms can move into an area very quickly, bringing rain or snow. Knowing what the weather will be like a few days before it happens is very helpful.

## Did You Know?

Alvin, Texas, holds the American record for getting the most rain in a 24-hour period. It rained 43 inches in Alvin on July 25–26, 1979!

**Meteorologists** study Earth's climate and weather. They use special equipment to take measurements of weather conditions. They use technology to make predictions about the weather. Weather predictions are called **forecasts**.

Meteorologists use weather maps to predict the weather.

Weather forecasts are important for many reasons. Meteorologists find out what kind of weather is coming. They study air pressure and wind to see if any storms are forming. If meteorologists see a storm forming, they can warn people in that area. They tell people if a dangerous hurricane or snowstorm is approaching. This helps people to plan ahead.

Some people need to know about the weather so they can do their jobs. Airport workers watch the forecasts to make sure it is safe for airplanes to fly. Firefighters use warnings about dry weather to stay on the lookout for forest fires.

Air traffic controllers use weather forecasts to direct airplane traffic.

# The History of Weather Forecasting

Thousands of years ago, weather forecasting was quite difficult. People tried to predict weather by looking at the clouds. Evangelista (ee van jil EE stuh) Torricelli (tor uh CHEL ee) invented the first weather instrument, called a **barometer**, in 1643. A barometer is used to measure air pressure.

A hand-drawn weather map from 1872.

Scientists began using weather maps in 1870. To make weather maps, scientists all over the country monitored the skies. They recorded the temperature, wind speed, wind direction, and air pressure. Then they sent this data to Washington, D.C. Scientists in Washington, D.C., used all this data to create weather maps by hand. It was a long, slow process. By the time they had created a weather map, the weather had already changed!

The first national weather service was the U.S. Army Signal Service. Years later, the U.S. government set up the Weather Bureau. Today, the National Weather Service (NWS) is our country's weather center. The NWS uses advanced technology to forecast the weather. Meteorologists working for the NWS study cloud patterns, wind, and temperatures. They try to predict possible outcomes of weather patterns.

A modern satellite image showing water vapor in Earth's atmosphere.

New technologies have helped scientists learn more about how weather happens. The first weather satellite was launched in 1960. It sent back the first pictures of Earth's atmosphere from space.

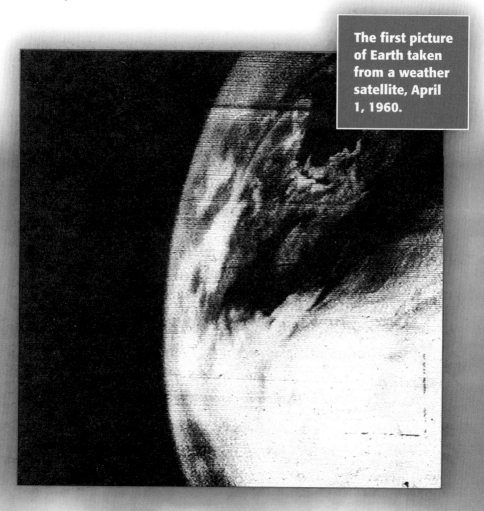

The first picture of Earth taken from a weather satellite, April 1, 1960.

TALK ABOUT IT

Why do you think improvements in satellite photography have increased the accuracy of weather forecasting?

# Modern Weather Maps

New technology allows meteorologists to record more accurate data readings. These readings help them predict what will happen in the atmosphere. Scientists collect all these reading and draw them on maps of the area. These drawings are called weather maps.

Rain

Snow

AM

Heavy Snow Possible

Rain

Snow

**Key:**

= Warm front

= Cold front

**L** = Low pressure

The maps often show wind direction and areas of high or low pressure. These two factors, as well as wind speed, predict where a storm will hit and how quickly to expect it.

Weather maps like this one help meteorologists predict the weather.

# Weather Fronts

Two of the most important symbols shown on weather maps are cold fronts and warm fronts. Cold air is denser than warm air, so it stays closer to the ground. When cold fronts move in under warm air masses, they can bring heavy storms.

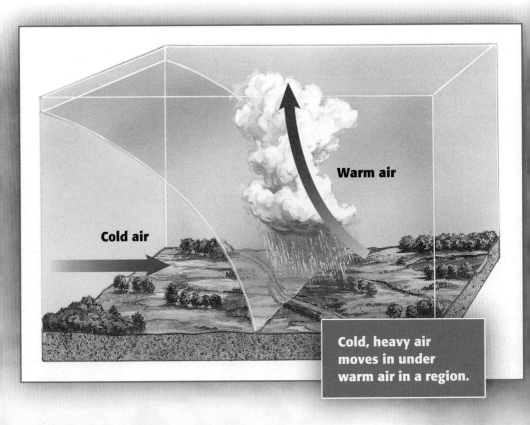

Warm air

Cold air

Cold, heavy air moves in under warm air in a region.

TALK ABOUT IT

A weather report on the radio says there is about a 1 in 4 chance that a cold front will move into your area. How could you write 1 in 4 as a decimal and as a fraction?

Warm fronts rise up and over cold air masses. Warm fronts can bring rain or snow that lasts for days.

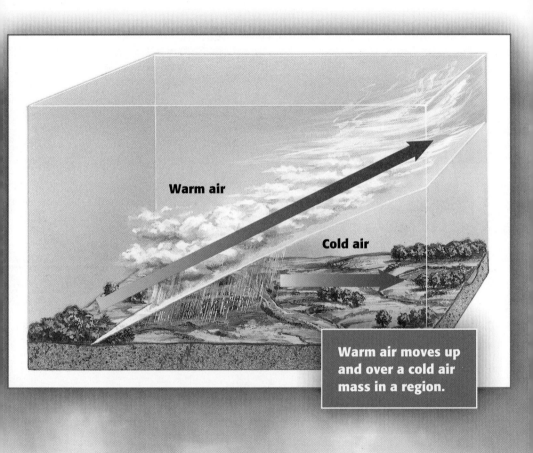

Warm air

Cold air

Warm air moves up and over a cold air mass in a region.

# Doppler Radar

Storms and other kinds of severe weather form very quickly. Meteorologists use technology to look for storm clouds. One important tool is Doppler radar.

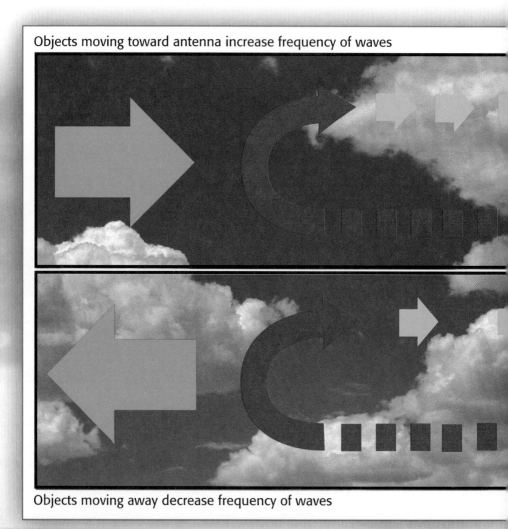

Objects moving toward antenna increase frequency of waves

Objects moving away decrease frequency of waves

**Radar** is a kind of technology that uses radio waves. Radio waves are transmitted into the atmosphere. The waves reflect off storm clouds and return to the radar station. Meteorologists use computers to make images of the reflected radio waves. They study these images to see the motion of clouds. This helps them track hurricanes, tornadoes, and thunderstorms.

Antenna sends radio waves.

Raindrops, other objects reflect radio waves

Did You Know?

Radar stands for RAdio Detection And Ranging.

# Weather Satellites

Satellites are devices that orbit Earth. They are
controlled by computers. They don't float away into
space because they are held in place by Earth's gravity.
Satellites carry special instruments that take images of
Earth. Satellite images are used to make maps and study
the weather. Satellite images can show amazing details
of Earth's surface.

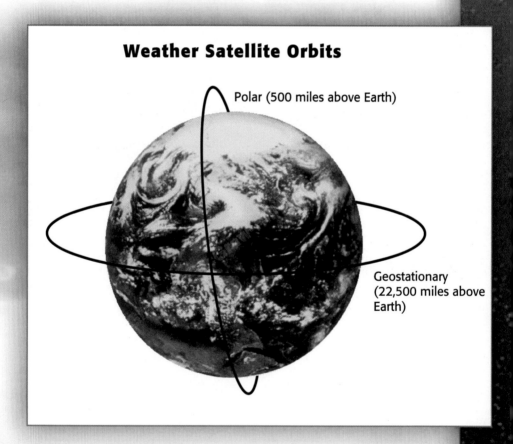

### Weather Satellite Orbits

Polar (500 miles above Earth)

Geostationary
(22,500 miles above
Earth)

Meteorologists use satellite images of clouds to look for storms. You might have seen satellite images of hurricanes on television. Tools aboard satellites help meteorologists predict storms long before they happen.

**Weather-monitoring equipment on NASA's Earth Observing System (EOS) Aqua satellite helps scientists forecast the weather from space.**

# Weather Symbols

Weather maps often use symbols to display a lot of information without using too much space. For example, cloud cover can be shown with symbols. Cloud cover is the amount of sky covered by clouds. Weather forecasters use terms such as clear, scattered clouds, partly cloudy, mostly cloudy, or overcast to describe cloud cover. Look at the table below to see the cloud cover symbols.

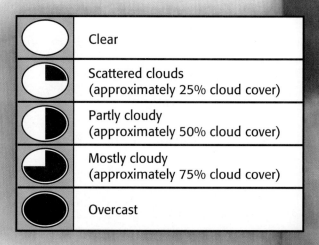

| Symbol | Description |
|---|---|
| | Clear |
| | Scattered clouds (approximately 25% cloud cover) |
| | Partly cloudy (approximately 50% cloud cover) |
| | Mostly cloudy (approximately 75% cloud cover) |
| | Overcast |

TALK ABOUT IT

If you saw the overcast symbol on today's weather map, how would you describe the likelihood of sunshine?

Wind speed and direction can also be shown using symbols. Flags and lines are the symbols for wind. A full flag (called a pennant) means that there is wind at 50 **knots**, a long line means 10 knots, and a halfline means 5 knots.

## Wind Symbols

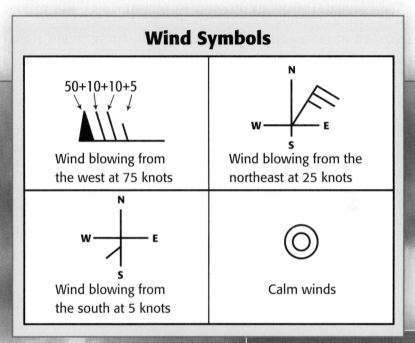

| | |
|---|---|
| 50+10+10+5 — Wind blowing from the west at 75 knots | Wind blowing from the northeast at 25 knots |
| Wind blowing from the south at 5 knots | Calm winds |

**Knots is the unit of measure for wind speed.**

# Severe Storms

A thunderstorm is the most common type of severe storm. Thunderstorms often form in **cumulonimbus** (kyoom yoo loh NIM buhs) clouds. These storms can cause huge electric sparks called lightning. The lightning heats the air and causes the noise called thunder. Thunderstorms usually bring heavy rains and strong winds. Some thunderstorms also produce hail.

Thunderstorms form when intense heat causes air to rise very quickly. As more of the heated air rises, it cools. Its water vapor forms clouds. Large amounts of water and ice crystals form in the clouds. Eventually, the upward draft of air cannot support the water, and it begins to rain.

## How a Thunderstorm Forms

Air cools

Warm air rises.

1. Strong updrafts form inside the cloud.

+ = Positive electric charge

– = Negative electric charge

Heavy rain

2. Electric charges build up inside the cloud.

Fierce thunderstorms can create even more dangerous storms, called tornadoes. A tornado is a violent, whirling wind that moves across the ground in a narrow path. Most tornadoes in the United States occur in the Midwest and South in an area known as Tornado Alley. Tornadoes are classified by the damage they cause. The stronger the wind, the more damage a tornado can do. A tornado's size is not directly related to its intensity. Small tornadoes can be very violent.

| The Fujita Scale | | |
|---|---|---|
| F-Scale Number | Wind Speed (mph) | Type of Damage Done |
| F0 | 40–72 | Branches break off trees |
| F1 | 73–112 | Moving autos pushed off the roads |
| F2 | 113–157 | Roofs torn off frame houses |
| F3 | 158–206 | Most trees in forest uprooted |
| F4 | 207–260 | Well-constructed houses leveled |
| F5 | 261–318 | Strong frame houses lifted off foundations and carried considerable distances |

The Fujita scale is used to report a tornado's intensity. The F-scale number is assigned after a tornado has passed.

Hurricanes are very large, swirling storms with low pressure at the center. They form over tropical oceans near the equator. Hurricanes are extremely dangerous. The strong winds of a hurricane stir up large waves in the ocean that can cause great destruction and flooding to areas along the ocean shores. Weather forecasters keep people informed as to when and where hurricanes will hit.

This satellite photograph shows Hurricane Linda.

# Glossary

**barometer**
> A device for measuring air pressure. *(page 6)*

**cumulonimbus**
> Puffy, flat-bottomed rain clouds that form vertically. *(page 20)*

**forecasts**
> Estimates about something that will happen. *(page 4)*

**knot**
> Wind measurement that is approximately 1.15 statute (nautical) mile per hour. *(page 19)*

**meteorologist**
> A scientist who studies the weather. *(page 3)*

**radar**
> Radio devise for finding distance and direction of objects. *(page 15)*